APQC'S PASSPORT TO SUCCESS SERIES

# Competitive Intelligence:

## A GUIDE FOR YOUR JOURNEY
## TO BEST-PRACTICE PROCESSES

**Farida Hasanali**
**Paige Leavitt**
**Darcy Lemons**
**John E. Prescott**

PUBLICATIONS

American Productivity & Quality Center
123 North Post Oak Lane, Third Floor
Houston, Texas 77024

Edited by Emma Skogstad
Designed by Fred Bobovnyk Jr

Manufactured in the United States of America

ISBN 1-928593-96-8

American Productivity & Quality Center
Web site address:  www.apqc.org

# Contents

# Acknowledgments

The American Productivity & Quality Center (APQC) would like to thank all of the organizations we have worked with to uncover the trends and best practices in the realm of competitive intelligence. Without the companies that sponsor our research—and especially those that are willing to impart their knowledge, experiences, and insights—we would not be able to share this valuable knowledge with the public.

We extend a special thank-you to those organizations that sponsored our six consortium benchmarking reports focused on competitive intelligence.

1. *User-driven Competitive Intelligence: Crafting the Value Proposition* (2003)
2, *Using Science and Technology Intelligence to Drive Business Results* (2001)
3. *Developing a Successful Competitive Intelligence Program* (2000)
4. *Strategic and Tactical Competitive Intelligence for Sales and Marketing* (1999)
5. *Managing Competitive Intelligence Knowledge in a Global Economy* (1998)
6. *Competitive and Business Intelligence: Leveraging Information for Action* (1997)

A number of these studies were conducted in partnership with the Society of Competitive Intelligence Professionals. The Institute for the Study of Business Markets also partnered with APQC in its competitive intelligence benchmarking efforts. John Prescott was a subject matter expert for all six studies; Jan Herring and Cynthia E. Miree also contributed at subject matter experts to individual studies.

APQC would also like to thank those that participated as best-practice organizations and allowed our study units to examine and learn from their competitive intelligence practices. A significant amount of information in this book was gained during those benchmarking studies.

# Preface

Ever since the American Productivity & Quality Center formed in 1977, our goal has been to disseminate knowledge to help organizations perform more effectively. We have done that in numerous ways over the years, from developing improvement and measurement approaches to offering benchmarking studies, conferences, training courses, research services, and a variety of publications.

Our members and other customers have expressed a need for easy-to-use resource guides in order to understand and implement programs and processes in a variety of functional areas. As a result, we have drawn on our experience and knowledge to produce APQC's Passport to Success book series.

We chose the title Passport to Success because these books are intended to guide you on what can be a difficult journey through somewhat foreign territory. Each book in this series provides readers with the mechanisms to gauge their current status, understand the components (or landmarks) of a successful initiative in a specific topic area, and determine how to proceed within their own organization.

The titles include:

- **Benchmarking**: *A Guide for Your Journey to Best-practice Processes* (2002)
- **Call Center Operations**: *A Guide for Your Journey to Best-practice Processes* (2000)
- **Communities of Practice**: *A Guide for Your Journey to Knowledge Management Best Practices* (2002)
- **Competitive Intelligence**: *A Guide for Your Journey to Best-practice Processes* (2004)
- **Content Management**: *A Guide for Your Journey to Knowledge Management Best Practices* (2003)
- **Customer Value Management**: *A Guide for Your Journey to Best-practice Processes* (2001)
- **Knowledge Management:** *A Guide for Your Journey to Best-practice Processes* (2000)

- **Stages of Implementation**: *A Guide for Your Journey to Knowledge Management Best Practices* (2000)

These books also supplement the other products and services APQC offers so that we may be your one-stop source for process improvement tools. To learn what else APQC provides in your area of interest, please visit our Web site at www.apqc.org or call 800-776-9676 (713-681-4020 outside the United States).

# Foreword

Competitive intelligence has a mystical allure shrouded in the romance of spying. As such, executives have responded in a variety of ways ranging from keeping a healthy distance from competitive intelligence for fear of being accused of espionage to naively embracing the tenets of Sun Tzu. Over the past seven years, our goal has been to systematically unveil the secrets of ethical competitive intelligence processes. Thanks in part to more than 25 best-practice organizations and the foresight of APQC, we have learned how to (re)design competitive intelligence processes that ethically deliver timely, actionable, and reliable intelligence to decision makers. In turn, the speed and quality of strategic and tactical decisionmaking improves, as competitive intelligence becomes an integral aspect of an organization's culture.

The distinguishing feature that differentiates the APQC series from most other research in the area was our conscious decision to focus on the "why" and "how" questions of competitive intelligence. Naturally, we are interested in what competitive intelligence functions are doing. However, we devote special attention to directly answering why they are doing what they are doing and how it is actually done. This approach allows us to develop thick descriptions and process models for many of the most critical aspects of developing an effective competitive intelligence function. For example, we learned how competitive intelligence processes begin and evolve over time to address the changing needs of managers. Our thick descriptions reveal competitive intelligence processes that have nuances characterized by indeterminacy and influenced by seemingly small events.

To continue the example, the launching of a competitive intelligence function is generally not what we consider to be a systematic process. Rather, an unpleasant event such as poor performance or an unexpected new product introduction by a competitor provides an opportunity for an intelligence function to emerge. We labeled this the "big bang." However, competitive intelligence champions must then generate sufficient, credible evidence to motive management to allocate resources to an intelligence function. Further, the champions need to demonstrate that an intelligence function has the ability to positively impact organizational outcomes. Even if management initially supports the development of a competitive intelligence program, its legitimacy and sustainability is not guaranteed. The road to effective competitive intelligence has many detours, curves, and potholes that must be successfully navigated to create an embedded intelligence culture.

Over the course of the APQC studies, at least three significant mindset changes have begun to occur in the intelligence profession. First, competitive intelligence is more than the intelligence cycle. The intelligence cycle is the process by which an intelligence request is initiated; data is collected, analyzed, and disseminated to intelligence users; and feedback is then provided to the intelligence group. Too often, competitive intelligence is equated to the intelligence cycle. Thus, many managers fail to appreciate the set of intelligence processes that are necessary to develop if their organizations are to have effective intelligence cultures. Second, national security intelligence and competitive intelligence need to inform and learn from each other. Until recently, there has been primarily a one-way flow of concepts, tools, and techniques from the national security community to the business community. Currently, the national security community increasingly recognizes that competitive intelligence practices are a valuable source of fresh ideas that complement their rich traditions. Third, and most important, the most valuable role of competitive intelligence is to in assist in the implementation of strategy and tactics. The mindset of focusing on implementation challenges the traditional myth that intelligence production and policy implementation are separate activities.

APQC's benchmarking studies on competitive intelligence have been instrumental in shaping the evolving mindset CI professionals. This is an important accomplishment.

There is little question that the APQC series is having a positive influence on the institutionalization of competitive intelligence in the business and governmental communities. However, we have another important challenge: influencing the academic community. Every decision-making model assumes the presence of information and intelligence. Yet, except in a rudimentary way, decision-making theory rarely incorporates the role of an intelligence function. Our hope is for academic researchers to explicitly incorporate the role of intelligence functions in their theories, thereby completing the symbiotic link between the academic, government, and business communities.

—John E. Prescott, Ph.D.
February 2004

# What is Competitive Intelligence?

Intelligence is not simply "nice to have." Rather, it is an integral part of decision making in both the business world and in our personal lives. Smart organizations know that to stay competitive, they must be able to anticipate and react to changes inside and outside of their industries. They also know that this requires having a plan for turning data into actionable intelligence from which strategically and tactically important decisions can be made. The use of such knowledge, called competitive intelligence, is now a core practice among leading organizations.

Providing quality competitive intelligence is not a random activity. APQC defines competitive intelligence as the systematic process of obtaining and analyzing publicly available competitor information to facilitate organizational learning, improvement, differentiation, and competitor targeting in industries, markets, and customers. The Society for Competitive Intelligence Professionals describes it as remaining cognizant of competitors' intentions and unanticipated marketplace developments by: scanning public records; monitoring the Internet and mass media; and speaking with customers, suppliers, partners, employees, industry experts, and other knowledgeable parties. Essentially, it is information, similar to

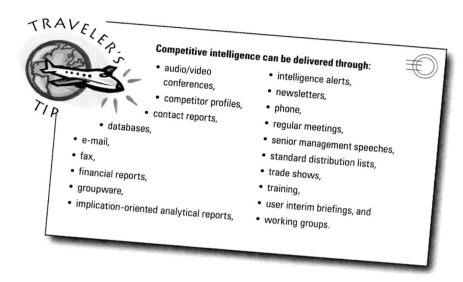

TRAVELER'S TIP

**Competitive intelligence can be delivered through:**

- audio/video conferences,
- competitor profiles,
- contact reports,
- databases,
- e-mail,
- fax,
- financial reports,
- groupware,
- implication-oriented analytical reports,
- intelligence alerts,
- newsletters,
- phone,
- regular meetings,
- senior management speeches,
- standard distribution lists,
- trade shows,
- training,
- user interim briefings, and
- working groups.

what journalists or researchers might retrieve, that the competitive intelligence function has analyzed for actionable implications.

More than simply allowing organizations to react to market developments, competitive intelligence can enable an organization to anticipate them. Competitive intelligence may be either strategic or tactical (that is, focused on the future or the present). Either way, competitive intelligence provides the knowledge and foresight to spot weaknesses and opportunities in both an organization's own strategy and that of its competitors. For this to occur, competitive intelligence providers must understand the differences in specific competitive intelligence needs, organizational goals, and the nature of decisions that result from organizational hierarchies. Conversely, intelligence users need to appreciate how intelligence functions operate.

The competitive intelligence function's primary job responsibility is to provide analysis with actionable implications. Making decisions based on this analysis then becomes the responsibility of the senior leaders or business managers. Ultimately, this valuable contribution elevates competitive intelligence from "stick-fetching" to decision making in the boardroom.

Operationally, this vision ideally involves the competitive intelligence function in business plans and tactical decisions and also provides training for all employees, a common competitive intelligence language spoken throughout the organization, and a mobilized competitive intelligence network. This is a challenging goal for any competitive intelligence professional to pursue.

To face this challenge, competitive intelligence providers must successfully develop a world-class competitive intelligence function with a request process, implications-focused analysis, knowledgeable clients, a central position in the organization's network, information technology enablers, value-added vendor relationships, and defined yet evolving product/service portfolios. The model includes five steps (Figure 1).

1. **Focus**—Develop a clear set of goals and objectives for competitive intelligence activities.
2. **Implement**—Cultivate an organizational culture conducive to implementing actionable competitive intelligence.
3. **Institutionalize**—Incorporate competitive intelligence practices into the daily activities of managers.
4. **Change**—Modify processes, behaviors, and performance in ways that help achieve organizational goals and objectives.
5. **Hone**—Make the competitive intelligence function a dynamic, evolving activity with a focus on continuous improvement.

## The Competitve Intelligence Process

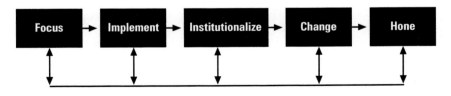

*Figure 1*

Landmark Two, Developing a Competitive Intelligence Program, will guide you through developing a focus and implementing a competitive intelligence effort. Landmark Three, Managing the Competitive Intelligence Function, will discuss how to institutionalize and modify your competitive intelligence function. And the final two landmarks will help you to hone the function's services and products to your organization's needs.

# Developing a Competitive Intelligence Program

Competitive intelligence involves developing implications, insights, and recommendations that are based on analytically combined intelligence, experience, credibility, and anticipation of the future.

Competitive intelligence functions need to produce value-added products that either reinforce or challenge current business practices. Competitive intelligence providers should view themselves as analysts whose job is to provide decision makers with not only recommendations, but also guidance and counsel to decision makers. Your credibility depends on your ability to anticipate key industry dynamics and assist in the development of actions plans. Furthermore, you should become embedded in the implementation processes of your organization. Competitive intelligence is as relevant for implementation as it is for formulation.

## DEVELOPMENT ISSUES

Developing a successful competitive intelligence function begins with the creation of the roles, administration, and structure of the function. This requires:

- initiating a program and developing the business case;

- developing the competitive intelligence vision, mission, and code of conduct;
- determining the key intelligence focus;
- cultivating a receptive culture; and
- selecting competitive intelligence personnel and determining required skills.

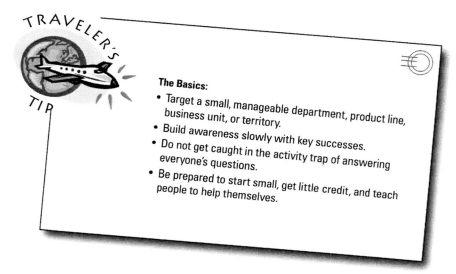

**The Basics:**
- Target a small, manageable department, product line, business unit, or territory.
- Build awareness slowly with key successes.
- Do not get caught in the activity trap of answering everyone's questions.
- Be prepared to start small, get little credit, and teach people to help themselves.

### Initiating a Program

During its benchmarking efforts, APQC has found that the beginning of a competitive intelligence effort is rarely an orderly, structured process. (For more on beginning a program, see the Stages of Development section of this landmark.) The process typically begins as a result of a critical incident and emerges over time after the formation of a functional unit.

Most writings in competitive intelligence literature outline a set of steps that should be followed to establish a competitive intelligence function. Although these steps are instructive, they fail to reveal how a competitive intelligence effort truly emerges over time. An emergent process, which is illustrated in Figure 2, was developed using data from best-practice organizations benchmarked by APQC in 2000.

# How a Competitive Intelligence Structure Emerges

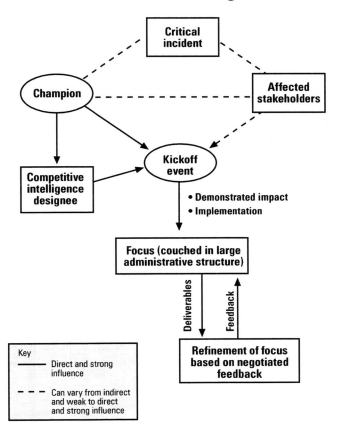

*Figure 2*

APQC has found that most competitive intelligence functions begin as a result of a critical incident. The source of the incident is not as important as the recognition that intelligence can assist in addressing the issue. Demand from senior management can also provide the motivation to start a competitive intelligence effort. A critical incident provides the opportunity to develop a competitive intelligence effort; however, a high-level champion has to emerge to provide the motivation and resources.

When forming the functional unit, you must demonstrate value and begin to develop plans for how it might be formalized in the organization. You will be tasked with developing an administrative structure and a set of processes for operations—essentially, a business case.

Your business case will detail the reason a competitive intelligence function is needed, the expected benefits, and the costs. Either the critical incident revealed how competitive intelligence can address existing problems, or senior management demand will drive the function's purpose. APQC has found at many organizations that the existence of the function is justified as a cost of doing business. In this case, it is critical to align competitive intelligence with your organization's overarching strategies.

Business case cost elements include:
- background and strategic context;
- evidence of need;
- potential benefits, outcomes, and indicators of success;
- organizational accountability for planning and design;
- initial investment required;
- resources and their source;
- technology support required; and
- project plans, including next steps, timeline, and deliverables.

While developing the business case, you will need to find a home for the competitive intelligence professionals. This may be in its own division or within market planning and research, R&D, information services, business development, or strategic planning. APQC has found that deciding where to house the competitive intelligence function is often based on where the initial critical incident occurred. If you are actually invited to determine where the function will reside, the appropriate location will become evident as you spell out the mission, key intelligence focus, code of conduct, budgets, initial products, and job descriptions. From there, reporting relationships begin to emerge.

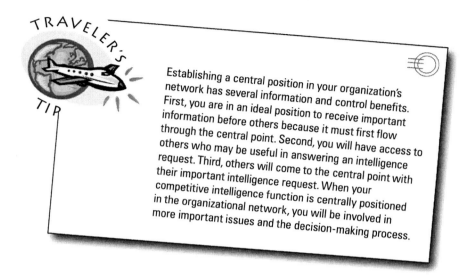

TRAVELER'S TIP

Establishing a central position in your organization's network has several information and control benefits. First, you are in an ideal position to receive important information before others because it must first flow through the central point. Second, you will have access to others who may be useful in answering an intelligence request. Third, others will come to the central point with their important intelligence request. When your competitive intelligence function is centrally positioned in the organizational network, you will be involved in more important issues and the decision-making process.

Once your competitive intelligence function is formalized, you can make a business case for continuing and upgrading on the basis of results achieved.

### Developing the Vision, Mission, and Code Of Conduct

Critical to your competitive intelligence function's stability is the establishment of boundaries of its efforts. Given that you will likely have limited personnel and other essential resources, your competitive intelligence function will need to have mechanisms to guide your undertakings. Some of the key boundary-setting mechanisms are a mission statement, code of conduct, and vision. Some best-practice examples follow.

The vision for competitive intelligence at Boehringer Ingelheim Pharmaceuticals Inc. is: "The Business Intelligence Unit enhances future competitiveness by producing intelligence that fosters well-informed executive decision making and supports formulation of strategies that preempt or neutralize those of our competitors. The Business Intelligence Unit reduces out corporate risk by increasing the awareness of competitive intelligence challenges and decreasing the element of surprise in our marketplace." And the function's mission is to:

- "produce and provide timely, actionable intelligence to our customers that supports the strategic business decision making of our company;
- to assess regularly with senior management the issues and threats or opportunities to our business and ensure the strategic impact of our efforts;
- to establish best intelligence practices across the company and facilitate intelligence efforts of company groups by developing and organizing the intelligence capability within those groups; and
- to integrate the intelligence collection and reporting functions within the company and ensure the compatibility of intelligence processes as well as communication and organizational tools across the company."

Shell Services International, on the other hand, simply states that its mission is: "Take SSI to a position of thought leadership in the application of competitive intelligence and knowledge sharing."

And at Telcordia Technologies, the mission of the competitive intelligence function is to:

- provide account teams with compelling factual arguments to neutralize competitors' advantages;
- provide product, marketing, and senior management with an accurate picture of competitor dynamics;
- create a high awareness of information protection;
- develop and maintain ethical intelligence guidelines; and
- train employees in collection and source development.

In the final example, at Glaxo Wellcome Inc., the competitive intelligence mission is: "Strategic Information/Competitive Intelligence identifies, acquires, analyzes, assesses, and communicates medical and commercial information and intelligence about our competitors in an efficient and ethical manner. These unique contributions facilitate decision making and provide a competitive advantage to Glaxo Wellcome."

Two sets of drivers influence the vision for your competitive intelligence function and serve as a reality check in developing it. First, marketplace dynamics act as early-warning indicators of what your competitive intelligence function is responsible for identifying. The second set of drivers consists of those that directly impact the way you perform your job. These drivers involve improvements in IT, new analytical techniques, changes in organization leadership, and new concepts.

### Determining the Focus

The focus of your competitive intelligence function and functional unit must be well defined. A well-articulated focus allows your competitive intelligence function to better leverage limited resources and develop an organization-wide understanding of expected contributions. The issue is not whether competitive intelligence has a strategic or a tactical emphasis, but rather that it can clearly articulate an emphasis. Focus competitive intelligence efforts on management areas that are critical to business operations and success. Some common areas of emphasis for competitive intelligence functions include:

- early warning,
- strategy formulation, and
- strategy implementation.

A process framework can provide a blueprint for how you will interact with internal clients. Think of this in terms of how intelligence requests will be handled. That is, how is competitive intelligence accessed, what roles do the producers and clients of intelligence play in answering the request, what products and services should the function offer, and what role do producers of intelligence play in the implementation of intelligence?

To answer these questions, solicit feedback, understand how the function might evolve, plan for global competitive intelligence capabilities, and spell out your own role in competitive intelligence. Priority setting allows you to politely decline requests, and referring keeps you in the good graces of internal clients. Your competitive intelligence function then has freed up time to focus on more highly valued intelligence products and services.

It is critical that your competitive intelligence function establish a realistic set of expectations. Promotional efforts that oversell and then do not deliver undermine the development of a competitive intelligence culture. Common sources of demand include unsolicited requests and events that occurred in the marketplace that require intelligence inputs to address. To address intelligence demands, your competitive intelligence function should develop a portfolio of products and services. To develop the function's portfolio of offerings, determine:

- what variety of competitive intelligence products should be offered to meet the needs of the organization's customers,
- what variety of competitive intelligence products should be offered to meet the needs of the organization's employees,
- what level of resources should be invested in each product,
- what benefits will be derived from each product, and
- if there are opportunities to partner with other units to design and implement a product.

Once the focus has been articulated, it needs to be communicated throughout the organization. Given limited time and resources, making trade-offs between providing a breadth of services and specializing in a few areas requires a keen understanding of the needs of the organization. Central to this decision is an understanding of the key goals and strategic initiatives of the company. By focusing on key business issues, your competitive intelligence function can assist managers in their jobs. This link to key areas of the company helps provide necessary resources, credibility, and access to key decision makers.

One way to conceptualize the portfolio is as a clothes closet. There are many types of clothes in people's closets, but they tend to wear a small set of them. However, on occasion, they need to wear swimsuits, formal wear, and yard work clothes. In the same way, you will likely spend about 80 percent of your time focusing on 20 percent of the portfolio; nevertheless, it is important to have the other 80 percent of the portfolio available when needed.

## Cultivating a Receptive Culture

Intelligence is an integral part of decision making. However, not all competitive intelligence clients understand its role and use. When clients become familiar with the function of intelligence through training, involvement in its development, and recognizing its impact on decision making, they become knowledgeable clients.

The development of a well-defined focus and the standardization of some competitive intelligence processes constitute the groundwork for cultivating a competitive intelligence culture. Viable and effective competitive intelligence functions develop varied ways to cultivate a culture receptive to the acceptance and use of intelligence. Reserve time to develop ways to cultivate this intelligence-oriented culture.

Your objective of cultivating a competitive intelligence culture is to institutionalize and embed competitive intelligence as a key process so that it has a high level of influence in decision making. Competitive intelligence is, above all, a social process. As such, its functions need a promotional plan; competitive intelligence providers need to let others know what intelligence is all about, the types of products and services potentially available, and how you can assist the organization in the development of an intelligence capability. Your promotional plans can take many forms, but should include:

- awareness-building training exercises such as lectures, scenario development, and demonstration projects, which allow the audience to better understand the role and capabilities of competitive intelligence;
- leveraging your high-level champion to ensure the function is visible and included in business plans;
- promotional materials that can be distributed to target clients in hard copy form or electronically;
- tangible rewards or recognition for individuals who provide intelligence;
- intelligence audits and key intelligence topic analysis to get individuals to focus on their important intelligence issues; and
- seeking out potential clients and meeting them on an individual basis to heighten their sensitivity to the value of competitive intelligence.

A requirement of a receptive culture is gaining clients' trust (Figure 3). Products and services that are perceived to be of high value create an atmosphere of trust and credibility with clients of intelligence. Trust results in clients requesting more, different, and increasingly sophisticated products and services. (For more on focusing on the users of competitive intelligence (i.e., the clients), see Landmark Five.)

## Building a Receptive Culture

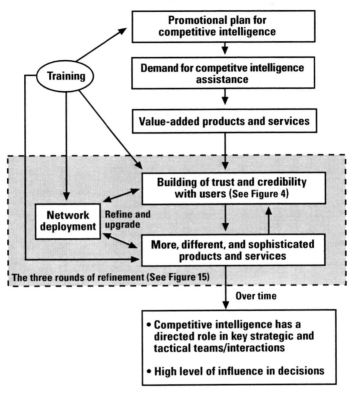

*Figure 3*

In APQC's 2000 evaluation of the outcomes of the intelligence activities, the competitive intelligence clients were most concerned with the degree to which competitive intelligence satisfied their needs, was actionable, and was delivered on time, as well the quality of the interactions with the competitive intelligence providers (Figure 4, page 16). The data also indicated that the products produced and the process skills of the competitive intelligence provider moderated the relationship among interactions with clients and their perceived evaluation of the outcomes. The quality of the

# Developing High-quality Interactions to Enhance the Trust and Credibility of CI Personnel

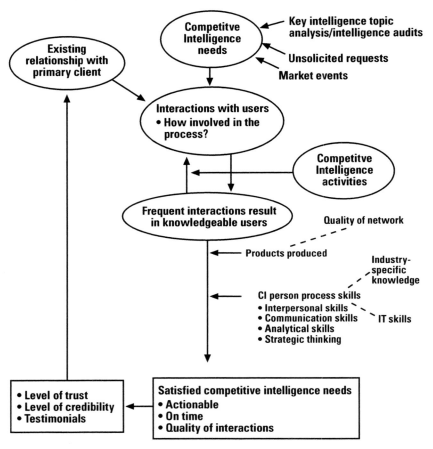

*Figure 4*

intelligence produced was somewhat influenced by the quality of the competitive intelligence provider's support.

The perceived outcomes of the intelligence assignment directly impacted the level of trust in the competitive intelligence provider, future intelligence assignments, and whether the client provided testimonials regarding the value of competitive intelligence. This process reveals that you can actively manage the development of credibility and trust by developing high-quality interactions with clients, providing products that satisfy their needs, and developing a set of process skills.

It takes anywhere from two to four years to develop a strong competitive intelligence culture. The process is never complete, however, because competitive intelligence efforts need to evolve over time if they are to survive.

### Selecting Competitive Intelligence Personnel

Appropriate personnel (e.g., managers, analysts, and information specialists) is critical to developing and refining competitive intelligence's role in the organization. As your competitive intelligence function begins to emerge and prove its business impact, it must justify its budget, including its need for resources. With often minimal staff and with the credibility of clients at stake, your competitive intelligence function must seek the right skills.

The amount of available resources, competitive intelligence focus, and specific project requirements typically dictate the size of the function's staff. Lack of resources to handle the demand frequently prevents competitive intelligence functions from allocating staff exclusively to strategic rather than tactical tasks; instead, competitive intelligence staff perform tasks necessary for projects shaped by the function's focus.

The key process skills required of a competitive intelligence provider are the ability to communicate, as well as interpersonal, analytical, and strategic thinking. IT skills, education, and experience—whether in industry, organization, or competitive intelligence—may also be important, depending on your function's focus. Other attributes include a strategy background, skills in using specific technology, intelligence training or background, and the ability to learn quickly.

It is up to your organization to decide whether you want industry-specific or organization-specific knowledge. You may find that educational requirements may be less important than people skills and experience.

Once you have a competitive intelligence staff in place, clearly define roles and responsibilities of individuals and departments involved in the knowledge-creation process. You will need to devote a considerable amount of time and thought to determine who does what where and when in respect to your competitive intelligence function. The process of determining roles and responsibilities is complicated because everyone in the organization, at least theoretically, engages in the creation of intelligence. If your function has successfully determined its focus, then it will have less conflict related to the implementation of roles and responsibilities.

With this understanding of the development issues involved, let's proceed with examining the stages of development.

## STAGES OF DEVELOPMENT

Development of a competitive intelligence function proceeds through four stages: preliminary start-up, start-up, establishment, and world-class operations.

At each stage of development, your competitive intelligence function should have an identifiable set of key activities or indicators that allows an organization to know its level of development (Figure 5). Once a competitive intelligence effort begins, three other aspects of the development sequence are important. First, a set of transition activities (Figure 6) enables your competitive intelligence function to move to the next stage of development. Second, there are outcomes that are associated with each stage. Third, there are events

## FIGURE 5: Development of a Competitive Intelligence Program: Key Activities Across Stages of Development

| Preliminary start-up | Start-up | Established | World-class |
|---|---|---|---|
| Knowledgeable CI personnel | **Demonstration project** | Developed IT, used as an interactive tool | **Embedded competitive intelligence culture** |
| Determine role of IT | Network design plan | Project-based competitive intelligence | **Dialogue-based CI** |
| Promotional plan | **Awareness training** | **Established product line** | **Integration of strategic and tactical intelligence** |
| **Identifiable champion** | Developing IT platform | **Consistent application of analytical framework** | **Direct role on key teams** |
| Preliminary administrative structure | Ad hoc requests dominate | *Coordination of all competitive intelligence activities throughout the company* | Simulations and modeling of competitive dynamics |
| Identifiable target of opportunity | *Intelligence audit to prioritize focus* | Formalized evaluation process | |
| | Informal feedback | **Network tuning of local champions** | |
| | **CI code of conduct** | *Knowledgeable and demanding clients* | |

NOTE: Bold activities are essential to be in a particular stage of development; italicized activities represent transition points.

## FIGURE 6: Transition Activities Between Development Stages

| | Outcomes | | |
|---|---|---|---|
| **Characteristics** | **Start-up** | **Established** | **World-Class** |
| Focus of uncertainty reductions | State uncertainty | Effect uncertainty | Response uncertainty |
| Focus of knowledge emphasis | Know what | Know how | Know why |
| Organizational outcome | Competitive awareness | Cooperative information flows | High decision impact flows resulting in intelligence-driven strategy and tactics |

that can lead to reversals in development or even the failure of a competitive intelligence function. (See traveler's tip.) This section briefly discusses each stage and its outcomes.

**Preliminary start-up phase**—A wide range of activities needs to occur in the preliminary start-up phase before a competitive intelligence function can be considered in the start-up stage of development. During the preliminary start-up phase, it is essential that a champion emerge from the ranks of senior management. As discussed earlier, a champion is needed to marshal resources and establish credibility. It is not so important that the champion understand all of the nuances of competitive intelligence but rather that he or she view competitive intelligence as critical to the long-term success of your organization.

TRAVELER'S TIP

**Intelligence Development Reversals And Failure**
Why do some competitive intelligence functions seem to lose their impact? Three underlying causes of intelligence reversal could diminish your function's reputation.

1. **Changes in senior management**—When the senior management of an organization changes, so do the fortunes of competitive intelligence. A new leader will have his or her own plans for the future. New leaders may intuitively see the value of competitive intelligence or may need to be educated regarding the value of competitive intelligence to preempt damaging cost cuts.

2. **A big mistake by the competitive intelligence function** (e.g., ethical missteps, early-warning error, and lowly valued products/service)—When a competitive intelligence function makes a major error or is consistently not satisfying the needs of intelligence clients, the credibility and trust in the function will diminish.

3. **Change in competitive intelligence function leadership**—When a competitive intelligence manager leaves, the unit is at a transition point. Competitive intelligence leaders have built relationships with intelligence clients, human intelligence networks, and competitive intelligence function dynamics that cannot be easily transferred to the next manager. Succession planning is important.

Conversely, those tasked with managing the competitive intelligence function must become subject matter experts in the field of competitive intelligence (if not already experts from previous experiences). Many tough questions regarding the costs and benefits of competitive intelligence will need to be answered in an authoritative way. During the preliminary start-up phase, consultants are often used to add credibility to the process. Also during this time, preliminary options related to issues addressed in the preceding section—including the mission, business case, promotional plan, and designation of roles—are developed. It is important to be flexible in the development of these issues.

One other activity of value is to begin to identify targets of opportunity: businesses, managers, and other potential clients that can benefit from an infusion of competitive intelligence.

**Start-up phase**—Budget-conscious managers will want to ensure that competitive intelligence will add value before committing significant resources to an effort that is not understood by most and may be feared by some. It is often wise to include your legal department in the promotional plan. Members of the legal department will be able to assist you in ensuring the competitive intelligence is legal and ethical. Share with them material related to the code of conduct.

As mentioned previously, a response to a critical incident is usually the beginning of a competitive intelligence function. A successful response has a few notable characteristics, such as being relevant to your business performance, including intelligence clients in at least one phase of the project (being realistic in terms of scope, timing, and objectives), and producing actionable intelligence.

Some potential clients will not appreciate the role of competitive intelligence. Whereas some will be supportive, others will consider you to be corporate spies. This is where it is critical for you to develop awareness of the value of competitive intelligence. One of the most important aspects of awareness building is to manage the expectation regarding what competitive intelligence can and cannot deliver.

Start-ups often suffer from a lack of focus and an emphasis on ad hoc requests. If your promotional plan is successful, then you will have more requests for intelligence than you can answer. Even if you limit your promotional efforts, satisfied clients will spread the word quickly. This is where determining your focus becomes critical.

During the start-up phase, IT platforms will be taking shape based on client needs, human intelligence networks will develop, and informal feedback will dominate the fine-tuning of your products and services. (For more on all three factors, see Landmark Three.) In the start-up phase, competitive intelligence efforts generally focus on reducing uncertainty and increasing your understanding of particular topics. This may involve questions related to assessing the competitive position of competitors, emerging market dynamics, and the alliance structure in an industry.

**Established phase**—You will know that you have an established competitive intelligence operation when three essential functions are in place.
- First, an established product/service portfolio is in place.
- Second, an established competitive intelligence function consistently adheres to its focus in addressing requests. Informal feedback still dominates but also now includes formal project evaluations and client surveys (discussed in Landmark Three).
- Third, there is a well-developed human network. Networks become critical to the collection of intelligence as projects become increasingly complex and cross functional (again, discussed in Landmark Three).

Two outcomes emerge from a competitive intelligence function in the established phase. First is the reduction of the impact of certain events, issues, and competitors' moves on your organization. Second is that high levels of cooperative information flow throughout your organization. IT will certainly facilitate the process, but a culture focused on competitive intelligence is critical.

There are two transitional indicators that signal movement to a world-class status. First, decentralized intelligence efforts are coordinated. Second, competitive intelligence clients become demanding regarding your products and services. These clients will actively participate in the intelligence process, incorporate intelligence into their decision making, and require intelligence from their coworkers regardless of level in the organization.

**World-class phase**—A world-class competitive intelligence function contributes significantly to bottom-line performance. There are three essential indicators of a world-class operation. First, competitive intelligence is coordinated and embedded in the culture of your organization, across geographical, cultural, and time barriers. Everyone talks and practices intelligence fundamentals, and there is an expanded network of colleagues that contribute intelligence. A second indicator, related to the first, is the integration of strategic and tactical intelligence. (More on this in Landmark Four.) Third, competitive intelligence providers play a direct role on key strategic and tactical functional units. In the world-class phase, the use of competitive intelligence is a way of doing business.

World-class competitive intelligence functions do not stand still. Transitional activities that lead to an even higher level of sophistication challenge the assumptions on which your organization bases its strategy and tactics, openly debating key issues to develop common mental models, and quickly responding to competitive dynamics.

World-class competitive intelligence functions focus on understanding the appropriate response to competitive dynamics and implementing those responses. This may involve knowing how and why to respond to a new product of a competitor; neutralizing its advantage while maintaining your advantage is an example of achieving a high level of response uncertainty reduction. The outcome is that competitive intelligence has high decision impact that results in an intelligence-driven strategy for the organization.

## CHECK YOUR STATUS

- Does your function have one or more senior-level executives to act as a key competitive intelligence champion?
- Does your function have a process for how competitive intelligence providers will operate?
- Does your function have clearly defined roles and responsibilities?
- Has your organization defined competitive intelligence and determined whom it will serve?
- Does your function have a seamless intelligence communication strategy within the organization?
- Has your function determined the process skills it seeks?
- Has your function determined the types of knowledge that are more valued?
- Has your function determined the importance of people skills relative to educational requirements in its competitive intelligence professionals?
- Has your function identified the roles of champions, networks, IT support, and training relative to competitive intelligence?
- Has your function set realistic expectations for itself? Has the organization?
- Has your function laid out a promotional plan?

# Managing the Competitive Intelligence Function

Managing your competitive intelligence function is a task in coordination and salesmanship. This landmark details the steps you will need to take in developing human networks, coordinating global efforts, guiding competitive intelligence activities, adhering to your focus, leveraging technology, evaluating the function's efforts, making improvements, and anticipating changes that will affect your competitive intelligence function.

## HUMAN NETWORKS AND GLOBAL EFFORTS

As your competitive intelligence function develops capabilities to address new demands, it will become evident that an active human intelligence network is required. Successful competitive intelligence functions develop and use decentralized, relationship-based human networks to leverage experience, expertise, and resources across their organizations. Whether tightly coordinated or decentralized in nature, internal and external human networks play a vital part in refining and upgrading competitive intelligence's role in the organization. Access to knowledgeable, responsive, and credible resources increases the function's ability to deliver timely, valued products and services.

**How to manage your competitive intelligence function:**
1. Be pragmatic. Conduct competitive intelligence in a practical manner aligned with company objectives.
2. Produce intelligence in a variety of formats or media so that managers have easy access to intelligence in their preferred format/medium.
3. Focus on the future. Direct attention to what tomorrow will be like and the implications for your organization.
4. View competitive intelligence from a global perspective. Although local knowledge is vitally important, emphasize on coordinating and integrating activities on a global basis.
5. Integrate formal and informal human networks. Traditional competitive intelligence literature emphasizes the creation of formal intelligence networks. You must understand and draw on a network of intelligence users and producers.
6. Develop and implement codes of conduct for company personnel and vendors. Be aware of differing ethical practices across the world and their potential impact on the competitive position of your organization.

There are two types of social networks.

The first type is composed of competitive intelligence colleagues that exist throughout an organization. Through a forum, dispersed competitive intelligence providers can meet on a regular basis to discuss emerging issues. Forums enable staff to interact; share best practices, experiences, and knowledge; and jointly solve problems. The forums can also support the development of new competitive intelligence functions throughout your organization.

The second type of network links the rest of your organization to the competitive intelligence function. This very critical network draws on pockets of expertise throughout your organization. Identify knowledge experts in each function of the organization, and incorporate into the competitive intelligence process as needed through cross-functional projects, guest speakers, conference calls, and informal discussions. The coordination of the diverse networks assists in the development of local competitive intelligence advocates.

There are a number of compelling reasons to coordinate human networks. First, diversified organizations have varied intelligence needs based on the different product-market arenas in which their businesses compete. Second, competitive intelligence providers are not experts in every function of a business, so they cannot be sensitive to the enormous variety of emerging competitive dynamics. Third, using networks allows your competitive intelligence function to leverage its resources, however limited. This means that your competitive intelligence function does not need to be large if it can draw on the expertise that resides throughout your organization. The breadth of intelligence is far greater, and the costs of tapping into these networks are significantly less than producing the knowledge from scratch. Fourth, networks eliminate silo mentalities so that people are involved in the formulation and implementation of proposed solutions. If they are part of the process, then implementation has a higher likelihood of success.

As the network facilitates the successful answering of intelligence requests, it enhances the building of trust and credibility in clients and the network participants. Over time, a competitive intelligence culture becomes embedded in the social fabric of the organization. The result is the placement of competitive intelligence personnel on strategic and tactical units where they have the capability to influence decision making.

It is important to remember that networks take time to develop and nurture. Begin in areas where the organization is developing its core capabilities and/or is experiencing its greatest competitive threats. When designing networks, you will choose between having a wide array of searching opportunities and the ability to transfer critical knowledge through networks. Tight or coordinated networks are usually small and consequently have limited search capabilities but strong knowledge transfer abilities. This is because smaller, tightly coordinated networks result in the development of strong ties among network players. These strong ties can be leveraged to transfer complex knowledge. Decentralized networks that have many weak ties spread across diverse players are excellent for gathering a lot of diverse data quickly but are weak in being able to transfer complex knowledge. Hence, the type of network that your competitive intelligence function builds should depend on the focus of its activities. A competitive intelligence function that is focused primarily on answering ad hoc requests will tend to develop a decentralized, loose network of contacts (Figure 7), whereas a competitive intelligence function that conducts in-depth projects on selected focus areas will have a small network of coordinated strong ties (Figure 8).

# Decentralized Network

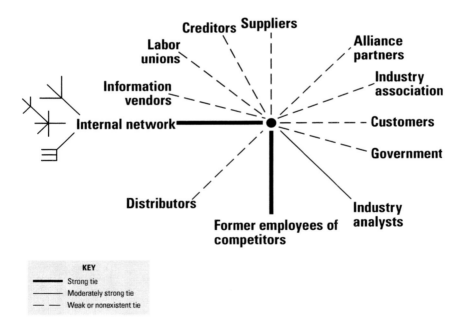

*Figure 7*

# Tightly Coordinated Network

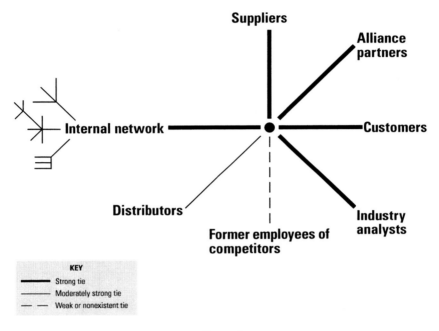

*Figure 8*

APQC has found five basic approaches for developing networks.

1. The recruiting approach emphasizes building a network in a systematic manner over time. Members of a competitive intelligence function often have as part of their job responsibility the recruitment of new members to their network. This is an aggressive approach to the development of a network. As part of the systematic approach, the competitive intelligence function will have established processes for recruiting and training network members.

2. Each competitive intelligence analyst/unit member develops his or her own network but shares it with other unit members in return for theirs.

3. Key stakeholders are included in any processes that can impact the organization's competitive position. This approach features a strong relationship between the competitive intelligence function and key stakeholders. Key stakeholders could be a business unit within the organization, an external vendor, a dealer, or government agencies.

4. Develop a network as the opportunity arises. In this approach, a competitive intelligence function typically develops relationships with the people who are working together on a project. The network expands with the number of projects completed. One of the important aspects of this approach is that network members may not be very active after a project is completed. However, the relationship developed during the projects can be used in the future to identify new members and serve as testimonials for potential members of the network.

5. Networks are built by the competitive intelligence function as it releases information to potential customers and requests feedback from them. Incorporating the feedback in the revised products and services leads to increased credibility for the competitive intelligence function and helps build a network of competitive intelligence contacts.

Often, specific groups are targeted for networks. For instance, corporate librarians provide a valuable link to the competitive intelligence process. Frequently, they are in separate units but need to work hand-in-hand with the competitive intelligence function. Coordinating and selecting vendors, as well as testing and administering IT systems, are often handled by the library.

Some competitive intelligence functions directly approach vendors when developing networks. Among best-practice examples, APQC has found that many leading competitive intelligence functions rely on customers, industry thought leaders, alliance partners, suppliers, and distributors within their networks. (Labor unions and creditors are used to a much lesser extent.)

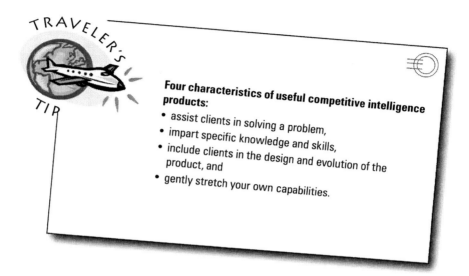

TRAVELER'S TIP

**Four characteristics of useful competitive intelligence products:**

- assist clients in solving a problem,
- impart specific knowledge and skills,
- include clients in the design and evolution of the product, and
- gently stretch your own capabilities.

One of the most fruitful targeted networks may be with the sales and marketing function. This is an opportunity not only to provide competitive intelligence, but also to gather intelligence. The sales function of an organization often provides a rich pool of information because of its frontline position with customers, as well as possible competitors, suppliers, and distributors. This network set-up allows for the continuous collection of valuable competitive information from primary sources, as opposed to more filtered, static public and secondary sources. Your ability to access these professionals can increase the richness of intelligence provided to the rest of the organization.

Developing and using networks of sales and marketing staff will also lead you to enhanced decision-making capabilities. As the marketplace becomes increasingly complex, your organization's proximity to its customers and your function's ability to detect, interpret, and respond to competitive conditions (e.g., competitive moves, customer needs, and marketplace dynamics) will lead to a sustainable competitive advantage.

*TRAVELER'S TIP*

Analysis should produce insights and occasionally the proverbial "aha." One of the essential features of analysis is that its outcome is context-specific. That is, a manager will often see different implications than a competitive intelligence provider. Be sensitive to this fact, and answer a request in a manner that identifies the implications for key outcomes. Samples of competitive intelligence analysis include:

- competitor profiling,
- core competency analysis,
- customer satisfaction surveys,
- financial statement analysis,
- industry scenarios,
- industry segmentation,
- issue analysis,
- management profiles,
- market signaling,
- mergers and acquisition analysis,
- portfolio surveys,
- strategic analysis, and
- value chain analysis.

Regardless of your approach, networks can help to coordinate units across your organization. The primary challenge is cultural: How do you design your competitive intelligence function so that it is responsive to a variety of national and cultural practices that exist in geographically dispersed companies? The larger the complexity, the more a sophisticated your network will need to be.

## ACTIVITIES AND ADHERING TO YOUR FOCUS

The central thrust of competitive intelligence is to "seed" the organization with a variety of products, services, and practices. Your competitive intelligence function should manage two related aspects of a high-impact "seeding" process. First, develop a portfolio of ways in which intelligence can be incorporated into the fabric of the organization. Second, ensure that the seeds have a set of attributes of value to managers.

**FIGURE 9: How Competitive Intelligence Supports Business Strategies and Initiatives**

| Competitive Environment | Future Options |
|---|---|
| • Identification of new opportunities<br>• Monitor competitor moves and countermoves<br>• Minimize surprises | • New competitive intelligence assignments |
| **Competitive Intelligence Users** | **Implementation Actions** |
| • Overcome organizational inertia<br>• Confirm existing opinions<br>• Expose blindspots<br>• Enhance strong relationships between competitive intelligence users and producers | • Identify constraints to successful implementation<br>• Assist in developing viable course of ongoing action<br>• Challenge/Test assumptions of implementation initiatives<br>• Assist in midcourse corrections<br>• Assist in evaluating the relevance and ramifications of competitive intelligence for initiatives |

A key issue is to deliver products and services that are consistent with what the organization uses. In the end, resources need to be devoted to those products that help achieve business objectives and strategies (Figure 9). However, as a change agent within the company, it is the responsibility of your competitive intelligence function to identify and develop new and different products that stretch organizational capabilities. If your competitive intelligence function is aware of the implications of important changes in the marketplace, then the products/services should assist clients in learning and adapting to the changes.

There is a vast array of products that a competitive intelligence function can produce, as shown in Landmark One. The most common categories are newsletters, databases, e-mail, training, and

| FIGURE 10: Products/Services Viewed As Effective By Users |
|---|
| In-depth intelligence assessments |
| Analytical alerts |
| Newsletters |
| Competitive intelligence Web sites |
| Ad hoc information searches |
| Participation on multifunction teams |
| Intelligence reports from human networks |

knowledge products such as implication-oriented analytical reports. Within each category, there are a variety of ways of delivering the product.

Figure 10 details common products, and Figure 11 details how to make those products client-friendly.

APQC has found that training, IT, and human networks produce the greatest degree of change in organizations. Each activity appears to strike an important chord. Training in an action learning context serves at least two purposes. First, it allows managers to

| FIGURE 11: Characteristics of Competitive Intelligence Deliverables That Drive Users To Action |
|---|
| • Quickly comes to the point |
| • Easy access |
| • Both electronic and face-to-face |
| • Personalized |
| • Relevant |
| • Factual |
| • Complete |
| • Blend of push and pull deliverables |
| • Experimenting with new deliverables on an ongoing basis |
| • Analysis and insight, not just summary |
| • Defined production schedule and delivery method |
| • Include commentary from key business partners |
| • Self-service options |

address an important business problem. Second, it develops the language of competitive intelligence in the trainees. On the other hand, IT has the potential to deliver a variety of competitive intelligence anywhere, anytime. In other words, IT collapses both time and distance. IT also provides an opportunity to create competitive intelligence.

When determining these activities, adhere to the focus you set in Landmark One. Given the limited size and resources of competitive intelligence functions, you cannot operate effectively if you are the hub of organizational requests for intelligence. It is common for competitive intelligence functions to become overloaded with ad hoc requests once the word spreads throughout the organization that they can help address intelligence needs. A priority-setting process establishes operating rules for the type of requests that are appropriate. Further, the request process establishes procedures for how the request will be executed. Intelligence audits and key intelligence topic identification are two widely used techniques for assisting in priority setting. Other criteria used include the degree to which the request includes analysis, whether others in the organization are more suited to address the request, and the willingness of the requester to fund competitive intelligence activities. When a request is denied, your competitive intelligence function should have alternatives for the requestor. The importance of a referral mechanism is twofold. First, the requestor may be someone your competitive intelligence function would like to include in its network. Second, as your competitive intelligence function evolves, the requestor may become a client.

## TECHNOLOGY

Action-oriented competitive intelligence functions develop IT approaches that address client needs, are flexible and simple to use, and allow fast communication across a diverse set of organizational members. One of the key challenges facing competitive intelligence functions is the development of IT systems that are efficient and effective. The wealth of publicly available information has lead to the proliferation of IT packages to collect, sort, analyze, and disseminate information.

Consequently, you must work in close contact with IT specialists, vendors, and corporate librarians to develop cost-efficient and effective systems. The cost and expertise necessary to implement state-of-the-art technology support is likely prohibitive for your competitive intelligence function to undertake on its own, except for relatively minor applications. Additionally, IT is evolving at a pace that requires expertise for successful implementation.

# IT's Role in Competitive Intelligence: Key Processes

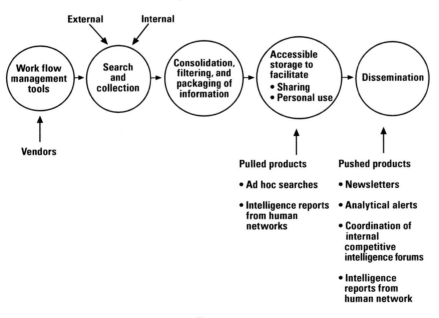

*Figure 12*

Essentially, IT should set competitive intelligence free, not enslave it. Figure 12 shows the key processes of IT as it relates to competitive intelligence. Key tools follow.

- Use work flow management tools to design an IT process appropriate for your function's needs. One of the primary values of a work flow management tool is its ability to search for and collect information efficiently so intelligence requests can be answered quickly. In other words, IT should enable people to quickly locate information sources, whether it comes from print sources, multimedia, or other people. This often requires the development of a knowledge warehouse to consolidate, filter, and package information and intelligence. The sophistication of a knowledge warehouse is less important than the information contained within it. IT should also allow easy access for employees outside of your competitive intelligence function so that they can use the information themselves and share it with colleagues. Access, however, needs to be tempered with security issues.

- Coordinate systems to maximize the effectiveness of the knowledge transfer process through intranet systems (Figure 13, page 38). APQC has found that the most effective intranet platforms for competitive intelligence provide:
  - competitive alerts,
  - easy-to-use discussion forums,
  - intellectual capital databases related to organization experts,
  - databases that catalog the variety of purchased and commissioned studies that exist throughout the organization,
  - the opportunity to purge unwanted data, and
  - the ability to coordinate diverse information systems.

# Intranet Framework

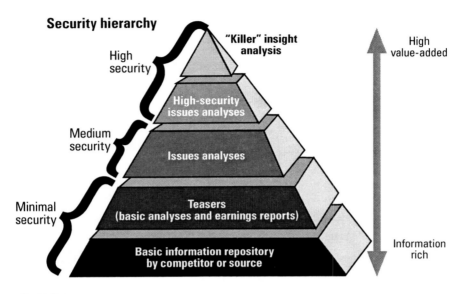

Source: Compaq

*Figure 13*

- The last key feature is the most critical and the most commonplace. Develop a Web site for your competitive intelligence function. Superior sites are differentiated by a specific set of attributes. A brief set of such attributes follows.
  - **Ease of navigation**—If a Web site is to be used by intelligence clients to perform some of their own intelligence work, then the site must be client friendly. Little, if any, training should be required for an intelligence client to find the information needed or to request assistance.
  - **Ability to archive**—One of the earliest uses of IT for intelligence providers was archived reports and intelligence sites. A well-developed archive system allows competitive intelligence providers and clients to easily search and retrieve material, which frees time for you to concentrate on analysis and implications.

- **Learning modules**—There is still a shroud of mystery surrounding the intelligence field. One way to debunk the myths of intelligence is for individuals to become more familiar with the roles and techniques of intelligence. A side benefit is that some individuals will want to actively participate in competitive intelligence processes. Learning modules provide a self-paced way for anyone in the organization to study topics in the intelligence field.
- **Portals to other areas within/outside corporation**—Often, all the intelligence client needs is a brief summary with implications. On other occasions, intelligence clients want to see the details of a particular study, article, or Web site. Links to internal and external sites facilitate the access to intelligence and free time for the intelligence producer.
- **One-stop access**—Intelligence clients do not want to traverse multiple sites to find the intelligence activities within their organization. A competitive intelligence Web site should provide one-stop access to all intelligence-related activities.
- **Security**—Intelligence can be considered one of the competitive weapons of a organization, so ensuring security of intelligence dissemination is essential.

## MEASUREMENT

Because competitive intelligence is one of many factors that contribute to a decision, it often is difficult to assess the direct impact of competitive intelligence inputs. The dual criteria of increased speed and quality present unique challenges to a competitive intelligence function. When a competitive intelligence function is focusing on speed, it functions similar to a news service; that is, there is a time value to intelligence, and those who obtain it first will receive the highest benefits. On the other hand, a focus on quality places the competitive intelligence function in a position similar to an advertising agency; that is, do we believe the claims presented to us by the intelligence operation? The trust and credibility that are essential to establishing believability are fragile and must be earned over time.

How your competitive intelligence function is evaluated can drive its evolution or dissolution. You can assess the impact of competitive intelligence products and services through a formal and/or informal evaluation process.

Because competitive intelligence efforts are viewed as overhead in most organizations, you may be interested in how your function is assessed by key clients. Drive your own formal evaluations. Use a wide variety of evaluation approaches that span individuals, products and services, and your competitive intelligence function and then determine the impact of competitive intelligence on the organization. Informal evaluations will then occur through interactions with clients. These evaluations will help you to understand their needs through face-to-face interactions (and less through technology-enabled communications).

Informal evaluations from the competitive intelligence audience are fundamentally more important to the evolution and survival of your competitive intelligence function than formal evaluations. Clients often provide ad hoc feedback regarding the value of competitive intelligence products, how they can be enhanced, and desires for new products. This feedback is often through e-mail or through the use of competitive intelligence in speeches, decisions, and discussions without explicitly acknowledging that it is occurring. This continuous stream of evaluation results in a continuous improvement process that is characterized by ongoing midcourse corrections.

## MAKING EFFORTS TO IMPROVE

APQC has found in best-practice examples that the competitive intelligence function is dynamic and evolving. A reason for the flurry of activity to continuously improve and hone the function is its relative newness for organizations; they do not always know what works and what does not. Also, the function must evolve to keep up with the changing demands of clients and the external environment.

A successful competitive intelligence function recognizes its own limitations. Address those limitations as soon as possible to advance the presence of competitive intelligence in your organization (Figure 14). Issues pertaining to funding, resources, IT enablers, culture, and prioritization will present the greatest challenges.

Actively target areas for improvement. This may be bolstered by client feedback, ideas learned from other organizations, or brainstorming. It is also important to determine how your organization will change as it uses competitive intelligence.

## Evaluation and Evolution Process

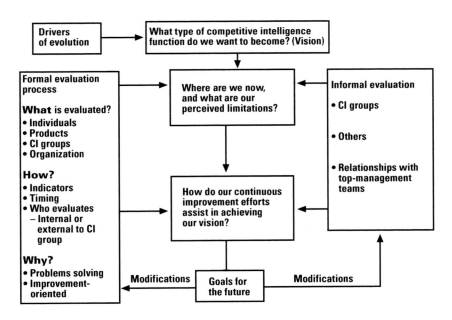

*Figure 14*

| FIGURE 15: Three Rounds of Refinement | | | |
| --- | --- | --- | --- |
| | **Round 1** | **Round 2** | **Round 3** |
| **Focus of activities** | Stick fetching | Prioritization and analysis | Direct role on key strategic and tactical teams |
| **Champion's role** | Foot in the door | Customer | Partner |
| **Network** | Up to two key informants and dozens of weak ties | Three or four key informants and scores of weak ties | Five to seven key informants and hundreds of weak ties<br><br>Central position in a cross-organizational network |
| **Information technology**<br><br>**Collection and distribution** | Awareness oriented | Knowledge warehouse<br><br>Facilitate and share access to CI | Manage the 24 time zones worldwide |
| **Training** | Basics of competitive intelligence<br><br>Data collection | Analysis | Simulations and modeling |

Figure 15 illustrates how the focus of competitive intelligence activities, the role of champions, the structure of networks, the application of IT, and the role of training change over three rounds of upgrading and refinement. You use this table to determine where you are positioned and where you need to direct attention in the future.

Outsource activities that are better or more appropriately performed by others. Often, vendors specializing in collection or customized analysis can help your competitive intelligence function use its time more efficiently. Vendors can free up time to allow your competitive intelligence function to spend more time developing interpersonal relationships with your clients and network.

## ANTICIPATING CHANGES

Successful competitive intelligence functions evolve over time to meet the changing needs of diverse clients. As the value of competitive intelligence is being recognized by more individuals, the demand for competitive intelligence services will expand. The ability of your competitive intelligence function to recognize and respond to changing needs is critical for their continued success.

One key to evolving while retaining stability is having experienced employees. Effective competitive intelligence functions change over time to meet organizational needs yet retain continuity through well-respected individuals and "cultural" acceptance of their contributions.

 **CHECK YOUR STATUS**

Has your function:
- developed active human intelligence networks?
- targeted specific groups for intelligence collection?
- coordinated networks locally and globally?
- developed tools to disseminate intelligence products, services, and practices?
- activated IT as the conduit of intelligence distribution?
- created a Web site for client activities?
- assessed the impact of competitive intelligence inputs?
- implemented a system for continuous analysis and improvement?

# Coordinating Actionable Intelligence

As the use of competitive intelligence increases within your organization, tailoring competitive intelligence products to each client's needs becomes more important. To be effective, you need to know how to coordinate requests, how to distinguish types of intelligence, and how it will be used. (Figure 16 is an example from a best-practice organization APQC has researched.) To explore this complex business process, this landmark identifies how to coordinate competitive intelligence at both the strategic and tactical levels and then how to manage the unique demands of technological intelligence.

## Application-focused Intelligence Work Flow

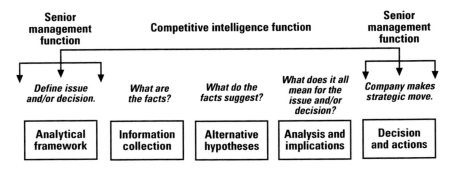

*Figure 16*

## STRATEGICAL AND TACTICAL INTELLIGENCE

Action-oriented competitive intelligence functions have a strong link between tactical and strategic competitive intelligence, so it is important to understand the differences.

Strategic intelligence is focused on the future and allows an organization to make informed decisions concerning impending marketplace and/or industry developments. Essentially, it deals with how your organization can create and respond to change in its industry and helps senior management map out your organization's future direction. Ultimately, over time, strategic intelligence facilitates significant organizational learning.

Tactical intelligence, on the other hand, is focused on the present; it relates to the implementation of your organization's current strategy. This level of intelligence can provide senior management with the information necessary to monitor changes in your organization's current environment and help it search for new opportunities; but it primarily supports activities in functional units. Tactical intelligence is real time in nature.

Consequently, there is a natural tension between strategic and tactical intelligence processes and implications. Senior management needs specific, strategically focused intelligence. At the same time, professionals in functional units such as R&D need tactical intelligence to assist in developing business and solving problems. So how do competitive intelligence functions provide both effectively? To maximize the potential benefit of competitive intelligence, the strategic and tactical levels must be coordinated. (Figure 17 provides an example of coordinating strategic and tactical intelligence with the sales and marketing functions.)

View the relationship between strategy and tactics as a circular process in which the two feed, challenge, and reinforce each other (Figure 18, page 48). The communication of key intelligence topics from both levels assists in the coordination and integration of intelligence, which creates this symbiotic relationship. Coordinate the intelligence through human networks, the development of

# A Process Framework for Coordinating Strategic and Tactical Intelligence in the Sales and Marketing Functions

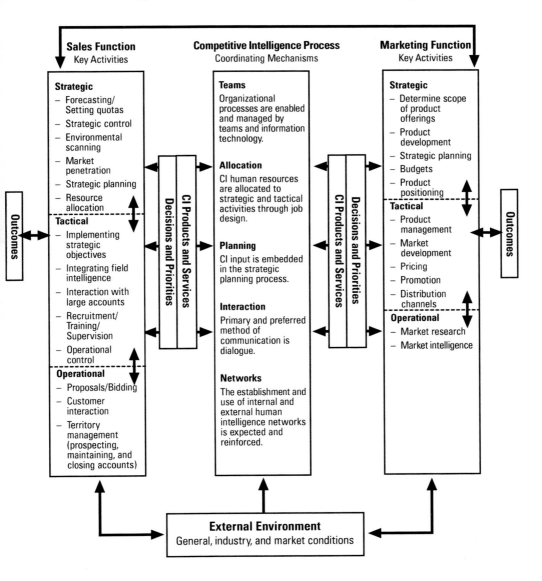

*Figure 17*

# Tactical Model Comparison

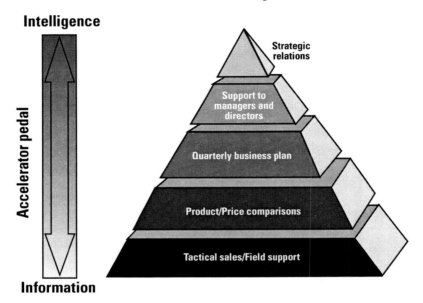

*Figure 18*

referral groups that can undertake intelligence projects that are outside the scope of a competitive intelligence function's mission, and cross-business issues that require competitive intelligence attention.

During a benchmarking effort in 1999, APQC found that coordinating strategic and tactical intelligence was an extremely high priority for the worldwide exploration business group business intelligence team (BIT) at Amoco Corp. Because of the fine line between strategic and tactical intelligence, the BIT believes it is important to coordinate the two as much as possible. The BIT work functions include business and competitive assessment at a strategic level and scouting and reporting on a more tactical level. Competitive intelligence provided by the BIT includes developing an industry perspective and an assessment of the competitive environment in context with its strategic planning process to provide competitor assessments and a country or regional perspective for country-level business planning efforts.

Coordination between strategic and tactical intelligence is also a high priority for MetLife's competitive intelligence unit. It is demonstrated by the strategic and tactical information senior management requests. In addition, MetLife's environment is such that no significant marketing decision is made without considering both strategic and tactical competitive information.

And at SBC Operations, APQC found that the competitive intelligence function, at one time, was organizationally structured so that an internal customer would have one contact for strategic competitive intelligence requests and another contact for tactical requests. The function found this formalized distinction too rigid. The artificial wall hindered the flow of information and confused internal clients. Information would also often fall between the cracks. Accordingly, the function minimized the formal distinction between the two types of intelligence when dealing with its customers and has come back to the synergy of a larger sharing operation.

## FOCUSING ON TECHNICAL INTELLIGENCE

Although the same set of underlying principles apply to all types of intelligence—regardless whether it is science and technology, market, competitor, or manufacturing intelligence—science and technology intelligence is unique in several ways that warrant attention (Figure 19, page 50).

Science and technology intelligence involves a unique liaison role of uniting managers and scientists that may use different business jargon. For example, managers are interested in cash flow projections, market growth rates, and industry profitability. Scientists, on the other hand, are interested in the latest developments in their specialty areas, recent publications in the technical literature, and intellectual discussions related to future

| FIGURE 19: What is Unique About Science and Technology Intelligence? | | |
|---|---|---|
| **Context of STI** | **Unique Character of STI** | **Operationalization Issues for STI** |
| **Liaison role** between managers and scientists | Need to understand the **technology watch process** and **network development process** | Develop appropriate **technology watch efforts** |
| Focus on **substitute products** and **technologies of competitors** | Understand the role of the **early warning process** | Focus on **early warning efforts** |
| One or more steps removed from **commercial products** | Understand the **commercialization link process** | Provide input to **commercialization teams**; become known as **STI content expert** |
| **Limited resources and skills** available to the firm | Understand the role of **competitive landscape** | Develop portfolio of **analytical tools** |

scientific breakthroughs. Both groups also differ in their time, interpersonal, and goal orientations. For instance, scientists tend to have long-term perspectives and value discovery over commercialization efforts. Managers have a more immediate focus, work on projects in a variety of areas, and value commercialization.

Science and technology intelligence often focuses on emerging technologies, where it may be difficult to even identify competitors and competitive dynamics. Traditional planning techniques do not work well in this situation. Instead, the identification of key assumptions and testing those with yet-to-be-created data is the preferred planning approach.

The choice of an overall science and technology intelligence design is critical because science and technology decisions involve large expenditures, are not easily reversed, and may lock an organization into a path for years to come. The design of a science and technology intelligence function provides guidance and structure to R&D managers, new product development units, strategic planning, business development, senior managers, and others in terms of science and technology alternatives and options in the context of their industry.

| FIGURE 20: The Four Models of STI Programs | | | | |
|---|---|---|---|---|
| **Model** | **Managing Technological Substitution** | **Technology Portfolio Management** | **Commercialization** | **Crafting Strategic Direction** |
| **Description** | Participation in an established technology while establishing a foothold in an emerging technology | Juggling multiple technological thrusts across time and stages of development | Create viable products with existing technologies | Provide just-in-time STI into the emergent strategy development process |
| **STI Input Focus** | Balancing exploitation and exploring substitution | Early warning of technological pipelines | Opportunities for exploitation | Ongoing emergence of opportunities and threats |
| **Outcome Focus** | Protection | Acquisition | Leveraging existing technologies | Interfaces of protection, acquisition, and leverage |
| **Indicator of Effectiveness** | Ability of STI to foresee the direction and speed of technological substitution | Degree to which STI influences the structure of the R&D portfolio | Number of new businesses that are launched | Ability to predict and anticipate emerging technologies, products, and events |
| **Limitation of Model** | 1. High coordination costs of integrating two sets of STI<br><br>2. Politics of resource allocation process | 1. Trade-offs involved in creating a balanced portfolio<br><br>2. Costs of developing a trust-based network | 1. Entrepreneurial mindset<br><br>2. Traditional planning techniques do not apply when markets do not exist | 1. STI professionals need strong anticipatory skills<br><br>2. Push back from managers |

## Organization of Science and Technology Intelligence Programs

Select from four distinct models and one matrix to structure your science and technology intelligence function. Figure 20 summarizes the four science and technology intelligence models. A description of each follows.

**Technology intelligence matrix**—The technology intelligence matrix (Figure 21, page 52) is based on two key dimensions that map the role of a science and technology intelligence function: inputs and

# Technology Intelligence Matrix

| | | STI Inputs | | |
|---|---|---|---|---|
| | | **Early Warning** | **Strategy Development** | **Operational Decisions** |
| **Outocmes Related to STI** | **Protection** | | | |
| | **Acquisition** | | | |
| | **Leveraging** | | | |

*Figure 21*

outcomes. The technology intelligence matrix can be used as a diagnostic, analytical tool to evaluate the science and technology intelligence approach of your organization, as well as that of your competitors. Alternatively, it can be used as a managerial tool in designing or redesigning your science and technology intelligence function.

The first dimension, inputs, concerns the focus of science and technology intelligence activities. These activities can be directed to early warning, strategy development, or operational decisions. Whereas most science and technology intelligence functions contribute in all three ways, their efforts typically are not distributed evenly among the three.

The second dimension of the matrix, outcomes, concerns protecting, acquiring, and leveraging technologies. Protecting technologies involves ensuring that emerging technological approaches and/or competitor initiatives do not erode the competitive advantage of your organization. The acquisition of technologies involves identifying new technological opportunities and related strategic decisions, including if and how to develop the technologies internally, partnering with other organizations to develop technologies, and/or whether or not to purchase the technologies from another source. Leveraging technologies addresses issues such as using existing technologies to create new products, entering new markets, and/or combining multiple technologies for product or market development.

Placing science and technology intelligence products in appropriate cells and mapping those individuals and groups that receive the intelligence populates the matrix. The technology intelligence matrix explains the role of science and technology intelligence in driving business results in several ways. First, a visual map of science and technology intelligence products and clients reveals how activities in a particular cell in the matrix facilitate the actions of intelligence clients in another cell. The matrix also allows you to understand the strengths and limitations of current science and technology intelligence activities. Because it is unlikely that your function will cover all cells in the matrix (due to a variety of reasons, including limited resources, organization strategy, and the stage of science and technology intelligence development), the matrix highlights areas of technological vulnerability. For example, an organization may emphasize the acquisition of technologies and devote too little time to leveraging its current technological capabilities. Finally, the matrix facilitates possible scenarios, which enables predictions. For example, you could fill the matrix for a competitor to determine its emphasis on technology, how its science and technology intelligence activities are structured, and vulnerable areas in its technology strategy.

**Managing technological substitution model**—The managing technological substitution model focuses on balancing the exploitation of an existing set of technologies while exploring an emerging substitute technology. In this situation, the balancing act provides considerable uncertainty. On one hand, the existing set of technologies requires investment to protect an organization's market position. Often, the product portfolio based on the existing technology is very profitable. On the other hand, the emerging technology has the potential to replace a portion or all of the market. Typically, the technology platforms for the existing and substitute technologies are not compatible.

The primary science and technology intelligence questions need to be divided into two sets that are integrated in the strategy development process. For the existing technology, the science and technology intelligence questions focus on trends, competitor assessments, benchmarking, and operational intelligence that help drive decisions related to efficient competition. Thus, science and technology intelligence provides an interface between strategy development and operational decisions. For substitute technologies, the science and technology intelligence questions focus on early warning of technology evolution, potential and/or existing competitors, and scenario development. R&D portfolio managers need an early warning regarding the most promising areas for investment, evaluation of existing R&D investments, overall technological trade-offs, and opportunities to leverage any of the organization's technologies. Managers in strategy development need intelligence related to the speed and direction of substitute technologies to allocate scarce resources among the competing technologies. In this model, the interface is between early warning and strategy development.

Science and technology intelligence capabilities are developed to provide early warning and protect the organization. In other words, you protect existing profit streams while ensuring that the organization is not left behind if emerging technologies are accepted in the marketplace. The competing demands of this balancing act and the resulting political image of managers place the science and technology intelligence function in a key brokering role.

This model has a few limitations. First, coordination costs are high to integrate the two sets of science and technology intelligence. Second, the science and technology intelligence function can get inadvertently involved in the politics of resource allocation across competing technologies. Third, the high levels of uncertainty can lead to a feeling of paranoia because the organization is constantly under attack on multiple fronts.

**Technology portfolio management model**—The technology portfolio management model focuses on the acquisition and subsequent leveraging of a portfolio of technologies. In this situation, the technologies in the portfolio are typically in different stages of development and vary in relation, so the organization has to juggle multiple technological thrusts across time.

Competitors also manage a technological portfolio, so understanding the innovation process of competitors and their technology pipeline is essential. Because a technology and its spin-offs can result in many generations of products, it is essential to understand the history of the technological portfolios of competitors. One way to address this issue is the development of an intellectual portfolio database. One of the primary clients of science and technology intelligence in this setting is R&D management. This set of clients is concerned with the successful acquisition (development) of new technologies that have a high level of commercial potential. Given limited resources, the distribution risk across technologies has long-term consequences. A second set of intelligence clients in this setting is strategy development. As technologies move toward commercialization, science and technology intelligence is necessary to develop market and position strategies.

The essential science and technology intelligence capabilities in this setting require skills linking early warning in protection and acquisition of technologies to strategy development and leveraging. Assisting in the acquisition of a technology and providing science and technology intelligence to units charged with leveraging the technology are essential skills. One limitation of this model involves the high costs of developing and nurturing a trust-based network. Because scientists are a central component of networks in this model, issues related to sharing and/or protecting science and technology intelligence are critical.

**The commercialization model**—The commercialization model for a science and technology intelligence function focuses exclusively on exploiting existing technologies. In this situation, an organization has an existing technology or set of technologies that can be potentially leveraged or transferred into new products and/or markets. The primary questions focus on assessing market potential, technological feasibility, patent likelihood, licensing opportunities, and supply chain entry points. These assessments determine whether or not to move forward with further investments.

Science and technology intelligence capabilities are developed to provide early warning assessments of opportunities. The commercialization model emphasizes strategy formulation rather than the operational decisions related to implementation. Industries such as biotechnology and bioengineering often employ this model.

There are two significant issues for those operating a commercialization model. First, dealing with entrepreneurs, as these organizations do, may involve trials and tribulations. Second, markets for the new technologies often do not exist. Therefore, it is essential to have a discovery-driven planning process that focuses on testing the quality of organizational assumptions.

**Crafting strategic direction model**—The crafting strategy direction model's role in driving business results is to ensure that senior managers and other key units are aware of the threats to the organization's ability to sustain its strategy. In this situation, the speed of competitive dynamics requires you to be flexible and fast-acting. The variety of competitors and technologies coupled with the fast pace of moves and countermoves require just-in-time intelligence. However, investments are sticky, and science and technology intelligence functions in this setting need to integrate medium and long-term intelligence with their just-in-time orientation. Medium-term intelligence often resides in existing product configurations and new product introductions. Long-term intelligence is found in technology investment opportunities. The clients of science and technology intelligence in this setting differ across the three time horizons. Just-in-time science and technology intelligence related to "breaking news" is required by senior management to assess immediate competitiveness issues. Organized field intelligence, such as from a tradeshow, is required for medium-term marketing and business development units. Technology scouting provides long-term science and technology intelligence.

An essential science and technology intelligence capability in this setting is the need for multiple human networks that span the just-in-time, medium-term, and long-term intelligence needs. This type of setting does not often provide good news from an intelligence perspective. Therefore, much of the effort is devoted to early warning and oriented toward protecting the competitive position of the organization. This early warning is central to the ongoing strategy development process, and the acquisition and leveraging of technology is essential for a sustainable competitive position. Thus, quickly detected promising technologies can be targeted for acquisition and impact to the strategy development process. As part of the early warning efforts, intelligence regarding potential opportunities to leverage existing technologies helps maintain the status quo.

Two overriding limitations need to be addressed when implementing this model. First, you need to have strong anticipatory skills that provide high levels of precision. Second, you need to have an intelligence team with strong personalities because managers will likely give strong opposition.

### Starting and Refining a Technological Intelligence Program

A science and technology intelligence function will be most effective in organizations that strategically focus on technology. Technology-based organizations need science and technology intelligence to protect, acquire, and leverage their technologies. When technology is not a centerpiece of an organization's strategy, managers will not devote sufficient attention to the complex set of technology issues that a science and technology intelligence function will produce.

Figure 22 details key activities to set up a science and technology intelligence function, based on the stages of development detailed in Landmark Two.

A detailed technology assessment is a prerequisite to beginning a science and technology intelligence function. The technology assessment should be a basic case analysis that will frame key issues from a technology perspective. The case analysis should contain an assessment of the state of technology in the industry, technological profiles for major competitors, and the technological strengths and limitations of your organization. In rapidly changing industries, the case analysis will be valid for only a year or two. However, the purpose of the case analysis is to sensitize managers to technology issues, determine trajectory paths for technologies, determine the technology strategies of competitors, and assess your organization's relative position in the industry.

## FIGURE 22: Key Activities Across Stages of Development

| Prestart-up | Start-up | Established | World-class |
|---|---|---|---|
| Knowledgeable STI personnel | Demonstration project | STI Web page used as an interactive tool | Embedded STI culture |
| Determine role of IT | Human network design plan | Project-based STI | Dialogue-based interactions with STI users |
| Promotional plan | STI awareness training | Established STI product line | Integration of strategic and tactical STI intelligence |
| Identifiable champion | Developing IT platform | Consistent application of STI analytical frameworks | Direct role of STI on key teams |
| Preliminary administrative structure | Ad hoc requests dominate | Coordination of all STI activities throughout the company | Simulations and modeling of competitive dynamics |
| Identifiable target of opportunity | Intelligence audit process to prioritize focus | Formalized STI evaluation process | The sharing of STI has been incorporated in performance evaluations and reward systems |
| Selecting an STI model | Informal feedback from intelligence users | Network tuning of local champions | In general, individuals use STI in their daily jobs |
| Technology assessment | Job descriptions for STI personnel | Knowledgeable and demanding STI users | STI is a central part of the decision-making process in the organization |
| Code of conduct | Vendor relationships | A standard set of terminology and processes have been developed to facilitate the sharing of STI | Have a process for making STI explicit |
| | STI customer request and feedback forms | STI budget process | |
| | | Formalized technology watch program | |

Another factor is that science and technology intelligence may require expertise outside of the intelligence function. Science and technology intelligence providers cannot easily learn the specialized and often tacit knowledge that these individuals possess. You need to establish strong relationships with individuals, departments, and units that are critical to implementing a technology-based strategy.

Integrating science and technology intelligence into the decision-making process can be challenging. An inverse relationship exists in which more science and technology intelligence providers are likely to participate in tactical units than in key strategy units. There is an important distinction between briefing senior management and directly participating in senior management strategizing.

 **CHECK YOUR STATUS**

- Has your function developed communication and reinforcement strategies to coordinate strategic and tactical intelligence?
- Has your organization determined if it needs a science and technology intelligence function? If so, has it:
  — created a science and technology intelligence function that predicts and re-evaluates technical assets?
  — created an approach to evaluate competitors' technologies?
  — selected appropriate models to manage technology intelligence?
  — created a forum for intelligence providers and technical specialties to share knowledge, ideas, and goals? (And is management sensitive to these findings?)

# Attending to the Competitive Intelligence Audience

Competitive intelligence products are often simply handed over, with the recipients left to decide if and how the intelligence will be directed toward implementation initiatives. But organizational goals, limited resources, and the speed of competitive dynamics require an integrated approach. Because competitive intelligence functions exist to assist executives, sales, planning, manufacturing, and other functions within the organization, understanding how to develop effective, working relationships with the recipients is critical to both the application of intelligence products and the survival of your competitive intelligence function.

So far, this book has detailed gaining a better understanding of how competitive intelligence functions emerge, managing operations, the coordination of strategic and tactical intelligence, and the structure of science and technology intelligence. A focus on client-driven competitive intelligence is a natural extension by concentrating on the audience instead of the producers of intelligence. This landmark focuses on how to develop successful relationships with an audience and how competitive intelligence is actually used.

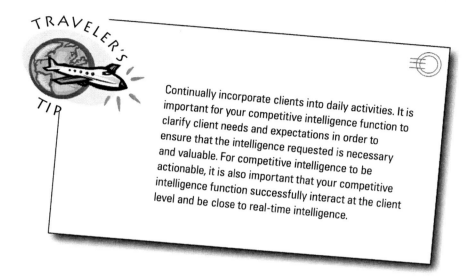

TRAVELER'S TIP

Continually incorporate clients into daily activities. It is important for your competitive intelligence function to clarify client needs and expectations in order to ensure that the intelligence requested is necessary and valuable. For competitive intelligence to be actionable, it is also important that your competitive intelligence function successfully interact at the client level and be close to real-time intelligence.

## DEVELOPING STRONG RELATIONSHIPS WITH CLIENTS

This section explores the attributes and processes by which you can establish, nurture, and maintain strong relationships with clients. The development of strong relationships with intelligence clients is a complex set of relationships among four factors.

1. **Competitive intelligence client characteristics**—Not all potential clients of competitive intelligence understand and/or value it. Some others are concerned that they put themselves in a vulnerable position if they rely on competitive intelligence providers for a significant part of their intelligence. Managers often collect their own information even when their organization has a formal intelligence process. Figure 23 details sources of vulnerability and uncertainty for potential competitive intelligence clients, and Figure 24 details characteristics that facilitate strong relationships. Your goal should be for your clients to understand that they need to rely on competitive intelligence providers for some part of their intelligence, share

| **FIGURE 23: Sources of Vulnerability and Uncertainty for Users of Competitive Intelligence** |
| --- |
| Clients must share their knowledge and the knowledge embedded in their networks as a key source of information to CI professionals |
| Clients must reveal confidential information to competitive intelligence professionals and rely on them to maintain confidentiality |
| Competitive intelligence professionals provide information that can be used to evaluate the quality of users' decisions |
| Client's knowledge of the environment depends on the efficacy of the intelligence provided by the competitive intelligence function |
| Inability to assess competitive intelligence implications |
| Inability to evaluate the quality of competitive intelligence work |

| **FIGURE 24: Characteristics of Competitive Intelligence Users That Facilitate a Strong Relationship** |
| --- |
| • Ability to accept or reject the validation provided by the competitive intelligence function and receptivity to changes in scope or perspective |
| • Ability to ask focused questions to meet specific business needs |
| • Ability to differentiate between useful and critical information |
| • An understanding that using competitive intelligence will help to achieve better results |
| • Candor |
| • Data driven/Fact-based mindsets |
| • Effective use |
| • Flexibility |
| • Intensely curious |
| • Need |
| • Partner in the design of competitive intelligence studies relevant to his or her areas |
| • Trust of the competitive intelligence professional |
| • Willingness to invest time in competitive intelligence |
| • Willingness to participate in the annual business planning process |
| • Willingness to provide "air cover" |
| • Willingness to review the rough cut of custom findings to hone the final report |
| • Willingness to share information |
| • Willingness to think beyond the company mindset |

confidential information with competitive intelligence providers, and share their own intelligence. Do your clients understand what intelligence is, why it is important, the need to work with competitive intelligence providers, and how to use the information? Participant involvement is the key mechanism for developing, nurturing, and maintaining positive client characteristics.

2. **Competitive intelligence function characteristics**—An appropriate structure and useful competitive intelligence products are critical for developing strong relationships. The following four characteristics of the competitive intelligence function are listed in order of importance for enhancing strong relationships with clients:
   - competitive intelligence products are important to the strategic and tactical thrusts of the organization,
   - the competitive intelligence function reports to high-level executives,
   - the competitive intelligence function has a clan-based culture rather than a hierarchical structure, and
   - competitive intelligence products are customized rather than standardized.

3. **Company characteristics**—Any template for developing strong relationships needs to be modified to the unique circumstances of each organization. Three characteristics prime for modification are organizational culture or personality, key performance metrics, and organizational structures that are informal and central.

4. **Competitive intelligence provider characteristics**—Characteristics of competitive intelligence providers are the primary factor for building strong relationships. Figure 25 shows important characteristics in competitive intelligence providers.

| **FIGURE 25: Characteristics in Competitive Intelligence Professionals** |
|---|
| • Have credibility and integrity |
| • Have referrals from satisfied competitive intelligence users |
| • Have the support of senior management |
| • Have an organizational rather than a individual orientation |
| • Have high levels of sincerity |
| • Have a willingness to reduce uncertainty for users |
| • Have high levels of competitive intelligence experience |
| • Produce competitive intelligence products/services relevant to current business issues |
| • Produce high-quality analysis |
| • Respect confidentiality |
| • Be congenial |
| • Be tactful |
| • Be timely |
| • Be dependable |

Use these four characteristics that influence the creation of strong relationships to assess your function's quality of relationships (Figure 26, page 66). To assess the factors that may benefit or impede a strong relationship with intelligence clients, you should:

- identify key attributes for each characteristic for the organization;
- evaluate the impact/importance for the development, nurturing, and maintenance of strong relationships;
- develop a matrix that classifies the attributes; and
- develop a plan of action based on the matrix.

Managers may not know how to design an effective competitive intelligence process, but they know one when they see it. Consequently, developing a strong relationship is not an end in itself. Rather, the development of strong relationships with intelligence clients creates several positive outcomes. Figure 27 (page 67) details a client-driven competitive intelligence model that depicts the causal flow from developing strong relationships to the

# Assessing the Quality of Relationships Matrix

**Time and Resource Needs for Remedial Action**

| | Low | High |
|---|---|---|
| **High** | **Priority Area** | **Monitor For Opportunities to Make an Impact** |
| **Low** | **Not an Emphasis** | **Ignore For Now But Monitor For Changes** |

*Impact/Importance for Strong Relationships*

*Figure 26*

desired objective of having intelligence clients and producers as cooperative producers, disseminators, and implementers of competitive intelligence.

### Dealing with Requests

The request initiates a set of activities involving clarification of the request, data collection, analysis, development of implications or recommendations, dissemination, feedback from clients, and ultimately implementation initiatives. On the surface, this process suggests that intelligence clients could be minimally involved with most states of the intelligence cycle. However, the greater the degree of involvement of intelligence clients throughout the cycle, the more likely that strong relationships will develop with competitive intelligence providers.

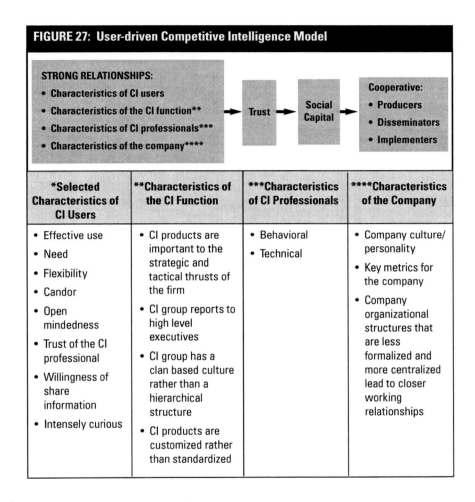

FIGURE 27: User-driven Competitive Intelligence Model

STRONG RELATIONSHIPS:
- Characteristics of CI users
- Characteristics of the CI function**
- Characteristics of CI professionals***
- Characteristics of the company****

Trust → Social Capital →

Cooperative:
- Producers
- Disseminators
- Implementers

| *Selected Characteristics of CI Users | **Characteristics of the CI Function | ***Characteristics of CI Professionals | ****Characteristics of the Company |
|---|---|---|---|
| • Effective use<br>• Need<br>• Flexibility<br>• Candor<br>• Open mindedness<br>• Trust of the CI professional<br>• Willingness of share information<br>• Intensely curious | • CI products are important to the strategic and tactical thrusts of the firm<br>• CI group reports to high level executives<br>• CI group has a clan based culture rather than a hierarchical structure<br>• CI products are customized rather than standardized | • Behavioral<br>• Technical | • Company culture/ personality<br>• Key metrics for the company<br>• Company organizational structures that are less formalized and more centralized lead to closer working relationships |

Clearly define the reciprocal and intertwined relationships among customer requests, feedback, and implementation of competitive intelligence project outcomes. Ill-defined competitive intelligence requests result in unfulfilled expectations on the part of the customer. Clients in turn implement few, if any, of the intelligence deliverables. The outcome for the competitive intelligence function is a loss of credibility and less influence in the decision-making process.

In terms of customer requests, clearly defining the scope of the project and deliverables is often a lengthy process. It is important to develop realistic expectations regarding the intelligence to be developed and how it will be used. Often, competitive intelligence personnel need to "push back" on the customer to refine their requests. Develop a competitive intelligence request form to specify the desired intelligence, deliverables, and time frame.

Also, have a plan of attack to answer an intelligence request. Spell out for the client what steps will be used in answering the request. Implicitly, this activity illustrates why the steps are important.

Two key aspects of establishing a plan of attach are standardization and transparency. Standardization means that the process will be followed consistently. It does not imply that all steps in the process will be done for every project, nor should it drive out creativity. Transparency means that others can easily understand how the process works. Transparency ensures that the process was appropriately implemented, thereby increasing the confidence clients attribute to the results.

It is unrealistic for intelligence clients to be intimately involved in all stages of the intelligence cycle for a variety of reasons, including relative expertise, time commitments, and job requirements. The key is to manage handoffs across stages in the intelligence cycle, be it in a consultative or partnering role.

A transition point is defined as a significant difference in the degree of involvement of either intelligence clients or producers across stages in the intelligence cycle. APQC has identified four transition points in the intelligence cycle.

1. **Project definition-data collection**—This transition is characterized by the reduced role of intelligence clients.
2. **Analysis-implications**—This transition is characterized by the involvement of intelligence clients.
3. **Recommendations-dissemination**—This transition is characterized by the reduced role of intelligence clients.
4. **Feedback-implementation**—This transition is characterized by the reduced role of intelligence producers.

During these transition points, ensure that intelligence clients have buy-in and are comfortable with the next set of steps in the intelligence cycle. Competitive intelligence providers who become skilled at managing handoffs across transition points in the intelligence cycle will build trust, social capital, and other positive outcomes.

There are two ways to speculate on the skills needed for managing handoffs. First, you can examine the set of skills necessary regardless of the type of transition. Second, you can look at the skills for each of the four particular transitions. Some of the skills and behaviors for maintaining strong relationships, regardless of the particular transition phase, follow.

- Convey key developments and bad news immediately.
- Schedule face-to-face appointments to explain data and analysis.
- Explain why clients should care about the transition information.
- Address client's questions directly without being asked twice.
- Convey why and how you might need to circle back in the project or how the project can be accelerated.
- Convey the information in clients' terminology, and walk them through relevant examples.
- Do more than required.
- Be true to the processes and politics of your organization.
- Be brief.
- Convey to clients how their skills, network, etc. can be best leveraged for a competitive intelligence project.

The second approach to examining the skills necessary during transitions is to examine each particular transition (Figure 28, page 70). This involves looking at a set of activities that can smooth each transition so that clients remain supportive of the intelligence. In this way, the competitive intelligence is more likely to be used.

### Feedback

Ongoing communication with clients and continuous process refinement through client feedback are critical to improving the speed and quality of decision making. Soliciting client feedback involves some very simple steps. Define deliverables at the onset of a project, after having clarified your clients' needs. Then, establish checkpoints throughout the project for a "status" meeting with the clients. At these meetings, hand off any interim deliverables and/or give an update on progress to date. This continual interaction

| FIGURE 28: Skills Necessary During Transitions | |
| --- | --- |
| **Transition phase** | **Skills** |
| Project definition ➡ collection | • Convey data needs for analysis.<br>• Convey how users can contribute data.<br>• Have users explain the meaning of data.<br>• Convey costs and time requirements for data.<br>• Convey what missing data means.<br>• Package data for analysis with users in mind.<br>• Convey ethical issues in collection.<br>• Convey difference between useful and critical information.<br>• Convey meaning of analytical frameworks. |
| Analysis ➡ implications | • Convey what analysis means and does not mean.<br>• Convey implications in the client's terminology.<br>• Convey differences between results and the conclusion.<br>• Learn to interpret analysis together.<br>• Learn to be interpretive rather than descriptive.<br>• Convey feasibilities and constraints of alternatives or recommendations.<br>• Convey why and how you might need to circle back in the project or how it can be accelerated. |
| Recommendations ➡ dissemination | • Assess a distribution list.<br>• Assess distribution model(s).<br>• Engage in two-way feedback.<br>• Assess urgency and criticality of competitive intelligence. |
| Evaluation ➡ implementation | • Assess the next steps for competitive intelligence.<br>• Develop metrics to measure implementation success. |

provides a way for you and your clients to stay on the same page and make sure that everyone is satisfied with and clear on the work being done. To stay abreast of current competitive intelligence issues and anticipate future issues, frequently communicate with senior managers to identify key issues and topics.

## THE CLIENTS' USE OF INTELLIGENCE

The extent to which competitive intelligence is actually applied will always vary. This is because the application of intelligence is not determined by the structure of your competitive intelligence function.

In addition to a number of factors like trust and relevance, a leading indicator of application is whether the intelligence is tactically or strategically focused. APQC has found that a tactical orientation is more conducive to directly applying the intelligence findings. The role of competitive intelligence during strategic implementation can be best characterized as "winning the negotiations," and the role of competitive intelligence during tactical implementation can be best characterized by "winning in the field." In the intelligence community, an accepted axiom is "facts in search of a question." This axiom refers to the belief that the same intelligence can be used to support points of view that are diametrically opposite. Those who can design the best arguments and are successful in persuasion consequently win the day. The term "winning the negotiations" reflects the fact that intelligence clients apply competitive intelligence during internal and external strategic debates to gain advantage.

For most people, it is easier to envision how competitive intelligence can be applied to tactical decisions and implementation initiatives, such as assisting sales to win a bid. Whereas a particular bid can be won, the more important issues are how over time a series of bids are won or lost, the moves and countermoves of competitors, and how clients' changing preferences impact product offerings.

This illustrates how competitive intelligence implementation at the tactical level assists in winning in the field on a daily basis.

There is significant opportunity here for you to be involved in additional areas of implementation. This may include procurement processes, counterintelligence, substitute products, suppliers, logistics or supply chain, and human resources practices. And it may involve:

- developing a human network to apply competitive intelligence findings;
- bringing to the attention of competitive intelligence clients important issues that might affect implementation;
- assisting in resolving the reliability of competitive intelligence developed during formulation;
- assisting in identifying the implementation capabilities of the organization;
- developing counterintelligence useful for implementation;
- assessing the legal, ethical, and public relations risks inherent in competitive intelligence activities;
- training in competitive intelligence activities related to implementation; and
- monitoring implementation initiatives to determine whether competitive intelligence does make a difference.

## MEASURING VALUE FROM THE CLIENT'S PERSPECTIVE

With the difficulty of pinpointing the return on investment for competitive intelligence, the development of strong relationships with intelligence clients lessens the need for formal/quantitative assessments.

A variety of methods are used to evaluate competitive intelligence projects. Consistent with the strong relationship approach, "soft feedback" in the form of unsolicited council, interviews or meetings with competitive intelligence clients, and e-mails are the popular methods. More formal methods such as written or electronic surveys, forms attached to competitive intelligence products, and focus groups are less used.

It is rare for competitive intelligence functions to be asked to quantify results. Possibly, the degree of quantification of competitive intelligence activities is inversely related to the sophistication of the competitive intelligence function, as well as the quality of strong relationships. The ability to anticipate competitor moves and minimize surprises and intelligence failures are key criteria appropriate for evaluating how well your competitive intelligence function assists during implementation initiatives.

Based on feedback to your competitive intelligence function, modify and refine competitive intelligence products to align them with the key issues facing the organization. Also, allow for the need to modify the competitive intelligence function's budget, staffing, mission, and reporting structure.

Soft feedback may be the preferred method of evaluation assessment, but it does not preclude the quantification of competitive intelligence's contribution. At the tactical level, identify where it is possible to track specific outcomes such as winning a sales contract and if it is possible to quantify the competitive intelligence contribution. One caveat is worth noting. Competitive intelligence is rarely the sole reason why a sales call is successful or customers are retained. When competitive intelligence is part of a unit, the unit's contribution can be quantified.

## CHECK YOUR STATUS

Has your function developed strong relationships with clients by:
- proving to clients that they can rely on your work?
- training clients on how they can apply intelligence?
- creating an appropriate structure and useful competitive intelligence products?
- modifying existing structures to the unique and evolving circumstances of your organization?

Does your function:
- assess intelligence provider/client relationships?
- provide an efficient process for dealing with client requests?
- promote client feedback and continuous improvement?

# About the Authors

**Farida Hasanali**

A project manager, Farida Hasanali has served in several roles at APQC. She has led and been involved in numerous consortium studies. Hasanali, whose expertise includes information technology and competitive intelligence, led the design and development of APQC's Knowledge Sharing Network. Hasanali coauthored APQC's Best-practice Report *Developing a Successful CI Program* and *Content Management: A Guide for Your Journey to Knowledge Management Best Practices*.

**Paige Leavitt**

An editor and writer, Paige Leavitt has helped to produce a number of APQC publications, including Best-practice Reports and the Passport to Success series. She is coauthor of *Capturing Critical Knowledge From a Shifting Work Force* and *Content Management: A Guide for Your Journey to Knowledge Management Best Practices*, as well as author of *Solving Problems in Schools: A Guide for Educators*.

**Darcy Lemons**

Darcy Lemons is a project manager with APQC. Lemons has led studies focused on best practices in competitive intelligence, e-learning, and knowledge management. Lemons was project manager for the consortium benchmarking study *Using Science and Technology Intelligence to Drive Business Results*. She is coauthor of *Capturing Critical Knowledge From a Shifting Work Force*.

## John E. Prescott

John E. Prescott is a professor of business administration at the Joseph M. Katz Graduate School of Business at the University of Pittsburgh (prescott@katz.pitt.edu). Prescott's research interests focus on dynamic competitive rivalry, alliance networks, technology strategy, and corporate governance. A specific focus is the design and implementation of competitive intelligence systems. He has published numerous articles in journals, and his teaching responsibilities include MBA, Ph.D., and executive courses in strategic management, competitive intelligence, and international management. Currently, he is the content expert for competitive intelligence benchmarking studies conducted by APQC. He was also the dean of the Business Analyst Program at Texas Instruments. Prescott consults internationally.

Prescott was a founder and the 1991-1992 president of the board of directors of the Society of Competitive Intelligence Professionals. He is a member of the Academy of Management, the Strategic Management Society, a past member of the editorial board of the *Academy of Management Journal*, and an international adviser of the Society of Competitive Intelligence, China.

# About APQC

An internationally recognized resource for process and performance improvement, the American Productivity & Quality Center (APQC) helps organizations adapt to rapidly changing environments, build new and better ways to work, and succeed in a competitive marketplace. With a focus on benchmarking, knowledge management, metrics, performance measurement and quality improvement initiatives, APQC works with its member organizations to identify best practices, discover effective methods of improvement, broadly disseminate findings, and connect individuals with one another and the knowledge, training, and tools they need to succeed. Founded in 1977, APQC is a member-based nonprofit serving organizations around the world in all sectors of business, education, and government.

Today, APQC works with organizations across all industries to find practical, cost-effective solutions to drive productivity and quality improvement. APQC offers a variety of products and services including:

- consortium, custom, and metric benchmarking studies;
- publications, including books, Best-practice Reports, and implementation guides;
- computer-based, on-site, and custom training;
- consulting and facilitation services; and
- networking opportunities.

## PUBLICATIONS

APQC is the preeminent source for cutting-edge organizational research and improvement information. Designed to ease your way to positive results, APQC publications come in many forms and cover a wide range of subjects.

### Passport to Success series

This low-priced series of paperbacks can guide you on what can be a difficult journey through somewhat foreign territory. Each book in this series provides readers with mechanisms to gauge their current status, understand the components of a successful initiative in a specific topic area, and determine how to proceed within their own organization.

*Knowledge Management: A Guide for Your Journey to Best-practice Processes* (2000)

*Call Center Operations: A Guide for Your Journey to Best-practice Processes* (2000)

*Stages of Implementation: A Guide for Your Journey to Knowledge Management Best Practices* (2000)

*Customer Value Management: A Guide for Your Journey to Best-practice Processes* (2001)

*Benchmarking: A Guide for Your Journey to Best-practice Processes* (2002)

*Communities of Practice: A Guide for Your Journey to Knowledge Management Best Practices* (2002)

*Content Management: A Guide for Your Journey to Knowledge Management Best Practices* (2003)

Other popular books include *Building a Breakthrough Business* (2004), *Capturing Critical Knowledge From a Shifting Work Force* (2003), and *If Only We Knew What We Know: The Transfer of Internal Knowledge and Best Practice* (1998).

### Industry-specific Collections

Using its award-winning benchmarking methodology, APQC aggressively and comprehensively researches practices critical to the corporate world. Through these efforts, APQC has formed an impressive catalog of case studies from the world's leading organizations. APQC offers these case studies, organized by industry, on its *Continuous Improvement* series of CD-ROMs. Individuals interested in their industry's continuous improvement efforts will find this collection useful in gauging industry-wide trends and examining best practices in a spectrum of continuous improvement arenas, from knowledge management and performance measures to competitive intelligence and online training. Collections are available for:

aerospace and airlines,

chemicals,

energy,

financial services,

food and beverage,

government agencies,

health care,

insurance,

pharmaceuticals and biotechnology,

technology, and

telecommunications.

## Best-practice Reports

This series of in-depth reports based on benchmarking studies consists of a detailed examination of study findings and case studies of leading organizations. Covering a wide range of topics in operational improvement, recent titles follow.

*Building and Sustaining Communities of Practice*

*Business-to-Business Branding: Building the Brand Powerhouse*

*Deploying Six Sigma to Bolster Business Processes and the Bottom Line*

*Improving Growth and Profits through Relationship Marketing*

*Improving New Product Development Performance and Practices*

*Managing Content and Knowledge*

*Managing Marketing Assets for Sustained Returns*

*Maximizing Marketing ROI*

*Measuring the Impact of Knowledge Management*

*New Product Development: Gaining and Using Market Insight*

*Performance Measurement: Implementing the Balanced Scorecard*

*Planning, Implementing, and Evaluating E-Learning Initiatives*

*Replicating Gains from Six Sigma and Lean*

*Retaining Valuable Knowledge: Proactive Strategies to Deal with a Shifting Work Force*

*Succession Management: Identifying and Cultivating Tomorrow's Leaders*

*The Customer-centric Contact Center: A New Model*

*User-driven Competitive Intelligence: Crafting the Value Proposition*

*Using Knowledge Management to Drive Innovation*

*Using Science and Technology Intelligence to Drive Business Results*

*Virtual Collaboration: Enabling Teams and Communities of Practice*

With many more to come in 2004

## The Profile Series

APQC has introduced a new series of reports that captures information on a specific organization over the course of several benchmarking studies. Unlike a report that simply indicates an organization's current perspective, this series details research from the early days of improvement efforts through to the organization's mature outlook as it experiences success. Readers have an opportunity to examine how an organization began its improvement efforts, how its focus evolved, and what challenges it faced. This is an excellent way to compare your own organization's improvement efforts.

Titles in this series include: *The World Bank Profile: Best Practices in Knowledge Management*, *The Dow Profile: Process-focused Best Practices*, and *The Xerox Profile: Best Practices in Organizational Improvement*.

## Performance Benchmark Series

The Performance Benchmark series of reports provide metrics results and key observations from focused benchmarking efforts. *Project Management*, the first report in this series, details compelling metrics data from 26 organizations that represent diverse groups of industries, structures, revenue classes, and project types. Metrics in this report concern project management professionalism, strategy, and methodology and processes. In addition to detail findings and a cross-tabulation of project management metrics, this report includes key definitions and the original survey's 25 questions.

Expect additional publications in this series concerning performance benchmarks in activity-based cost management and customer service.

Learn more about APQC publications at www.apqc.org/pubs.